Window Shopping

Finished size approx 17 inches by 13 inches by 4 inches.

Requirements

5 Fat quarters of patterned fabric

This is for the squares on the outside of the bag, bindings and the pockets inside.

From these 5 fabrics cut 24 pieces 3 1/2 inches square some from each colour.

From the remaining fabrics choose 2 for the inside pockets and cut a piece from each 16 inches by 8 inches.

1/2 metre of dark fabric

This is for the outer bag sashings, base and handles.

From this fabric cut 2 pieces 5 inches by 20 inches for the handles.

Cut 10 pieces 1 1/2 inches by 11 1/2 inches

Cut 16 pieces 3 1/2 inches by 1 1/2 inches

Cut 4 pieces 1 1/2 inches by 17 1/2 inches

Cut 1 piece 4 1/2 inches by 17 1/2 inches for the bag base
Cut 1 piece 4 inches by 17 inches for the lining base.

1/2 metre of patterned fabric

This is for lining your bag.

Cut 2 pieces 17 inches by 13 inches

1 metre of calico

1 metre of cotton wadding
I have used Warm and Natural

Threads for sewing and quilting

1. Layout your squares o... design you like. Place the dark strips between the squ...

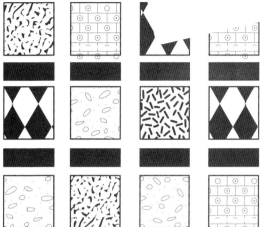

2. Sew together into 4 rows of 3 blocks with the 1 1/2 inch sashings in between using 1/4 inch seam allowance. Press seam allowance towards the sashing fabric.

3. Take the 1 /12 inch by 11 1/2 inch and place between the rows and one on each end

4. Sew rows together with 1/4 inch seam. Press seam allowance towards the sashing fabric.

5. Take the 1 1/2 inch by 17 1/2 inch pieces and add to the top and bottom of the panel. Press seam allowance towards the dark fabric.

Make two panels the same, they should now measure 17 1/2 inches wide by 13 1/2 inches high.

6. Take the 4 1/2 inch base panel and sew to the bottom edge of the side panels with a 1/4 inch seam allowance.

I have made my base in the diagram a different colour to show where it is.

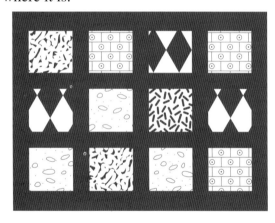

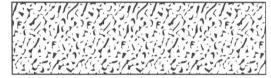

7. Cut a piece of wadding and calico slightly larger than your finished bag panel. Place the panel onto the wadding and calico, spray glue or baste together ready for quilting.

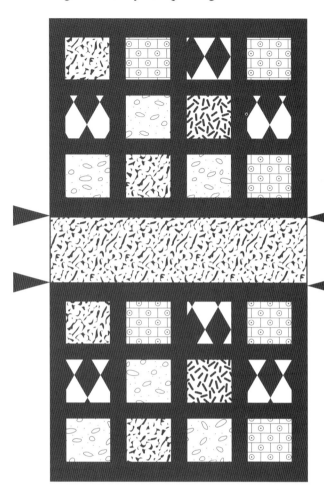

8. Quilt in the ditch along the base seams indicated by arrows on the diagram. This will give you a line to use later to form the base. Quilt panel as desired, I have quilted in the ditch around each square, 1/4 inch in down both sides of the sashings going down and across, using a hera marker and ruler I have quilted across the squares on the diagonal and 1/4 inch apart across the base.

9. Trim all excess wadding away from panel, I use my rotary cutter and ruler for this as it gives nice clean edge.

10. Fold bag in half across the base right sides together, carefully match the base seam, pin and stitch down both sides with a 1/4 inch seam allowance. Reverse stitch the top edge of the bag.

11. Take one of the bottom corners of the bag and match the side seam with centre base. Right side together.

This is the bottom corner section of bag.

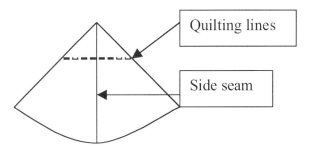

With the side seam on the top stitch across the quilting lines through the side and base to form the bottom of the bag. Do the same to the other corner. Corners can now be cut off leaving ¼ inch seam allowance.

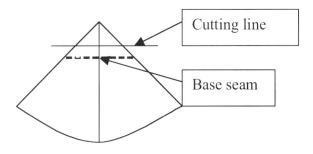

Turn the bag right side out.

12. Take the 2 inside pocket panels 8 inches by 16 inches, fold in half on the short sides, right side together, cut piece of wadding 8 inches square, place pocket panel onto the wadding. Stitch down the sides with ¼ inch seam. Clip the top folded corners away, this will give nice pointed corners when you turn the pockets right sides out. Press flat and quilt, if you have decorative stitches on your machine use them here to decorate the top edge and add strength at the same time.

Make both pockets the same.

13. Fold the lining panels in half to find the centre of the long sides. Mark with a pin on the bottom edge
Fold the pockets in half to find the centre of the bottom edge and mark with a pin.

Place the pockets on the right side of the lining panels matching the centre on the bottom edge. Pin pockets in place. Stitch down both sides of the pockets 1/4 inch in from edge, reverse stitch the top edge of the pockets for strength.

14. Add the 4 inch by 17 inch base to the side panels, press seam allowance towards the base panel.

15. Cut a piece of wadding and calico slightly larger than the lining panel spray glue or baste the three layers together the same as the bag panel.

Quilt across the base seams as before, quilt down the sides of the pockets. This is enough to hold the lining in place, if you want to do more it will look nicer.

16. Trim back wadding. Make up lining the same as the outer bag.

17. Take the two handle pieces, cut 4 pieces 3 1/2 inches by 5 inches from one of your 5 fat quarter pieces add these to either end of your handle pieces.

Press seam open.

18. Take your Handle strips and fold in half down the length right side out. Press fold.
Open out and fold raw edges into the centre fold you have just made. Press new folded edges.
Fold in half on original fold.
You should now have a strip a quarter the width of your original strip and with all raw edges hidden.
Stitch down the handle on the open edge first, then the folded edge. Add a few more lines down the centre or use a decorative embroidery stitch. The more stitching you do the stronger the handle will be.

19. Pin handles in place on the outside of the bag with the ends pointing up the bag. Machine in place, I always reverse over the handles to add strength.

20. Place the lining inside the bag, carefully pin around the top of the bag matching the side seams first, use lots of pins.
Machine around the top with 1/4 inch seam.

21. From one of your remaining fabrics cut 2 pieces 2 1/2 inches by 17 inches to bind the top of your bag.

Fold them in half down the length right sides out, press the fold.

Unfold and place them right side together and stitch across the short ends.

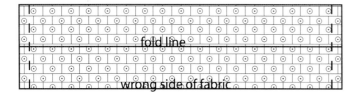

Fold the piece in half on the original fold line right side out. You should now have a hoop of fabric.

Place the hoop of fabric on the top of the bag on the outside with the raw edges together, line up and pin the side seams first. Pin around the top of the bag and make the binding hoop fit.

Stitch in place by machine with a generous 1/4 inch seam.

Fold binding hoop over the top and slip stitch the folded edge down to the lining covering any previous stitching.

Your bag is now finished.

Zen Bag
Finished size approx 15 inches wide by 11 inches high by 4 inches deep.

Requirements
6 fat quarters of contrasting fabrics
I have used the Zen range from Makower

½ metre of fabric for lining the bag.

1 metre of soft cotton wadding, I used dream cotton

1 metre of calico

Thread to match for sewing and quilting

Magnetic clasp

Choose 3 of your fat quarters for the rail fence blocks and cut the following pieces.

Fat quarter one and three
Cut 10 pieces 1 inch wide by 21 inches long, cut one piece 7 ½ inches by 18 inches this is for inside pockets. From each fabric.

Fat quarter two
Cut 10 pieces 1 inch wide by 21 inches long.
Cut 2 pieces 1 ½ inches wide by 21 inches long from these cut 12 pieces 1 ½ inches square

Fat quarter four

Cut 3 pieces 3 ½ inches wide by 21 inches. From these cut 34 pieces 1½ inches wide these are for sashing the blocks together on the bag fronts.

Fat quarter five

Cut one piece 4 ½ inches by 15 ½ inches for the base panel of the outer bag.
Cut one pieces 4inches by 15 inches this is the base panel for the bag lining.

Fat quarter six

Cut 2 pieces 6 inches by 21 inches for the handles

1.Take the one inch strips of fabric and sew together down the length with a 1/4 inch seam allowance in sets of three.
Make 10 sets

2. From these strips cut 96 pieces 2 inches square.

3.Sew together in sets of four. Make 12 units of each pattern.

4. Arrange in three rows of 4 blocks.

5. Sew sashing strips in between blocks with quarter inch seams. Press seam allowance towards the sashings

6.Take the remaining sashing strips and a sew together with the one inch squares in between.

Make 6 of these, press seam allowance towards the sashings.

7. Sew the sashing strips between the rows of squares. Make both bag panels the same.

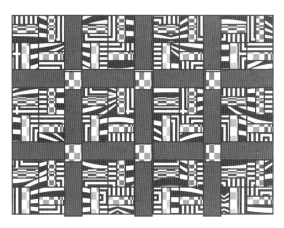

8. Press the panels well and add the 4 1/2 inch by 15 1/2 inch base panel to the bottom edges of your bag panels with a 1/4 inch seam.

9. Press seam allowance toward the base panel.

This is the bottom corner section of bag.

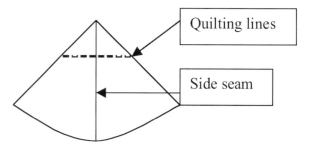

With the side seam on the top stitch across the quilting lines through the side and base to form the bottom of the bag. Do the same to the other corner. Corners can now be cut off leaving ¼ inch seam allowance.

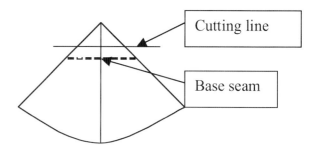

Turn the bag right side out.

Bag panel should now look like this.

10. Cut a piece of wadding and calico slightly larger than your bag panel.

11. Place panel on wadding and calico and spray glue or baste in place ready for quilting.

Quilt in the ditch along the base seams and down the sashings. I have also quilted on the diagonal across the pieced blocks. I used a hera marker and a ruler to mark the lines for quilting.

12. Trim all excess wadding away from panel, I use my rotary cutter and ruler for this as it gives a nice clean edge.

13. Fold bag in half across the base right sides together, carefully match the base seam, pin and stitch down both sides with a 1/4 inch seam allowance. Reverse stitch the top edge of the bag.

14. Take one of the bottom corners of the bag and match the side seam with centre base. Right side together.

15. Take the pocket panels and fold in half on the short side right side together, cut a piece of wadding to this size and place the folded pocket on top of wadding, Stitch down both sides with a 1/4 inch seam allowance. Clip off top of folded corners, turn pocket right sides out and press pocket flat, use something pointed to push out the corners.

16. Quilt pockets

17. From the lining fabric cut 2 pieces 15 inches by 11 inches.
Fold the lining panels to find the centre of the long sides mark with a pin on the bottom edge.
Fold the pockets to find the centre of the bottom edge.
Place the pockets on the right side of the lining panels, matching up the centre markers, pin in place. Stitch down both sides of the pockets reverse stitching at the top for strength.

18. Sew the lining base to linings with 1/4 inch seam allowance. Press seam towards the base.

24. Cut the ends of the handles on the 45 degree angle.

25. Find the centre of the handle and mark with a pin, measure 3 inches from the pin in both directions and put in another pin.

Fold this centre section in half down length and stitch in place between the pins.

place the handle on the outside of your bag with the ends facing up. Stitch in place by machine. Reverse stitch over handles to add strength.

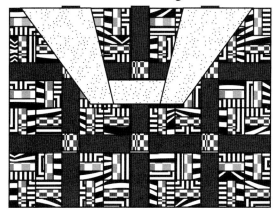

19. Lining should now look like this.

20. Cut a piece of wadding and calico slightly larger than the panel. Spray glue or baste the 3 layers together for quilting.

21. Quilt across the base seams as before, quilt down the sides of the pockets. This is enough to hold the lining in place, if you want to do more it will look nicer.

22. Trim back wadding. Make up lining the same as the outer bag.

23. Take your Handle strips and fold in half down the length right side out. Press fold.
Open out and fold raw edges into the centre fold you have just made. Press new folded edges.
Fold in half on original fold.
You should now have a strip a quarter the width of your original strip and with all raw edges hidden. Stitch down the handle on the open edge first, then the folded edge. Add a few more lines down the centre or use a decorative embroidery stitch. The more stitching you do the stronger the handle will be.

26. Place the lining inside the bag, carefully pin around the top of the bag matching the side seams first, use lots of pins.
Machine around the top with 1/4 inch seam.

27. From one of your remaining fabrics cut 2 pieces 2 1/2 inches by 17 inches to bind the top of your bag.

Fold them in half down the length right sides out, press the fold.

Unfold and place them right side together and stitch across the short ends.

Follow instructions for window shopping to bind top of bag.

Finish bag with a magnetic fastener and buttons.

Star Bright Cushion

Finished size 20 inches square
Requirements

5 fat quarters of fabric

Fat quarter of calico

Fat quarter of wadding

22 inch zipper

20 inch feather cushion pad.

Thread for sewing and quilting

Fat quarter 1 centre star and binding
Cut 4 pieces 2 1/4 inches by 21 for binding
Cut 1 piece 4 1/2 inches square
Cut 8 pieces 2 1/2 inches square

Fat quarter 2 large star
Cut 4 pieces 4 1/2 inches by 2 1/2 inches
Cut 4 pieces 2 1/2 inches square
Cut 8 pieces 4 1/2 inches square

Fat quarter 3 star background
Cut 4 pieces 4 1/2 inches by 8 1/2 inches
Cut 4 pieces 4 1/2 inches square.

Fat quarter 4 border
Cut 2 pieces 2 1/2 inches by 16 1/2 inches
Cut 2 pieces 2 1/2 inches by 20 1/2 inches

Fat quarter 5 cushion back
Cut one piece 20 1/2 inches by 18 inches

1. Take the eight 2 1/2 inch squares of fabric 1 and the eight 4 1/2 inch squares of fabric 2 and draw a line on the diagonal on the wrong side of fabric.

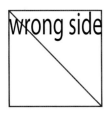
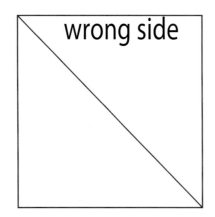

2. Take the 2 1/2 inch squares and place one on one end of the 2 1/2 by 4 1/2 inch fabric 2 pieces and sew on the diagonal line. Cut off corner leaving a 1/4 inch seam.

Press triangle over and add another square to the other side. Sew on line and trim as before. Press.

It should now look like this. Make 4 the same.

3. Take the 8 1/2 inch by 4 1/2 inch background pieces and the 4 1/2 squares for large star and do the same, make 4.

4. Layout star centre.

5. Sew together in 3 rows of 3 pieces with 1/4 inch seam allowance.

Gift Bags made using Makower Flowers and Makower Christmas Fabrics

Zen Bags Made in the new Zen Range of Fabrics From Makower.

Finished Size Approx 15 inches wide by 11 inches high by 4 inches deep
Made by Sarah Wellfair, Avril Knight and Helen Rymer

Star Bright Cushions made in Makower flowers range.

Finished size approx 20 inches square
Made by Sarah Wellfair

Square Drawstring Bag
Made by Avril Knight

Starbright Christmas Cushions
Made by Sarah Wellfair

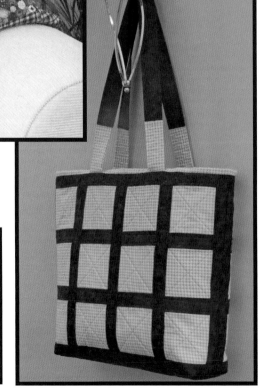

Window Shoppping bag
Made by Sarah Wellfair
Fabrics from Makower Flowers
range
Finished size approx17 inches wide
by 13 inches high by 4 inches deep

Press the seams on the centre row towards the middle square. On the outer rows press the seam allowance towards the outer squares.

6. Sew the rows together carefully matching the seams, if they are pressed in the right direction they should easily lock together. Press seams away from the centre.

7. Now layout the larger star using the small star as the centre square.

8. Sew together in 3 row of three as before and press seam allowances in the same direction as small star. Sew rows together.

It should now look like this, it should measure 16 1/2 inches square.

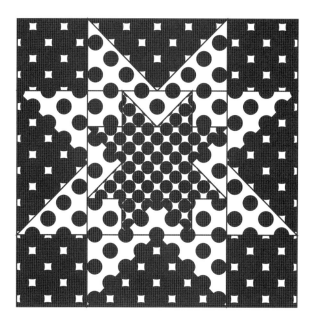

9. Take the 16 1/2 inch by 2 1/2 inch border pieces and add to top and bottom of star block. Press seam allowance towards the border.

10. Add the last 2 border strips to either side press seam allowance towards the border.

11. Place panel onto wadding and calico, baste or spray glue in place. Quilt as desired.

12. Trim back wadding and calico to edges of panel.

13. From your remaining fabrics cut a piece 5 1/2 inches wide by 20 1/2 inches long.
Fold one long edge in 1/2 inch and stitch down fold with 1/4 inch seam.

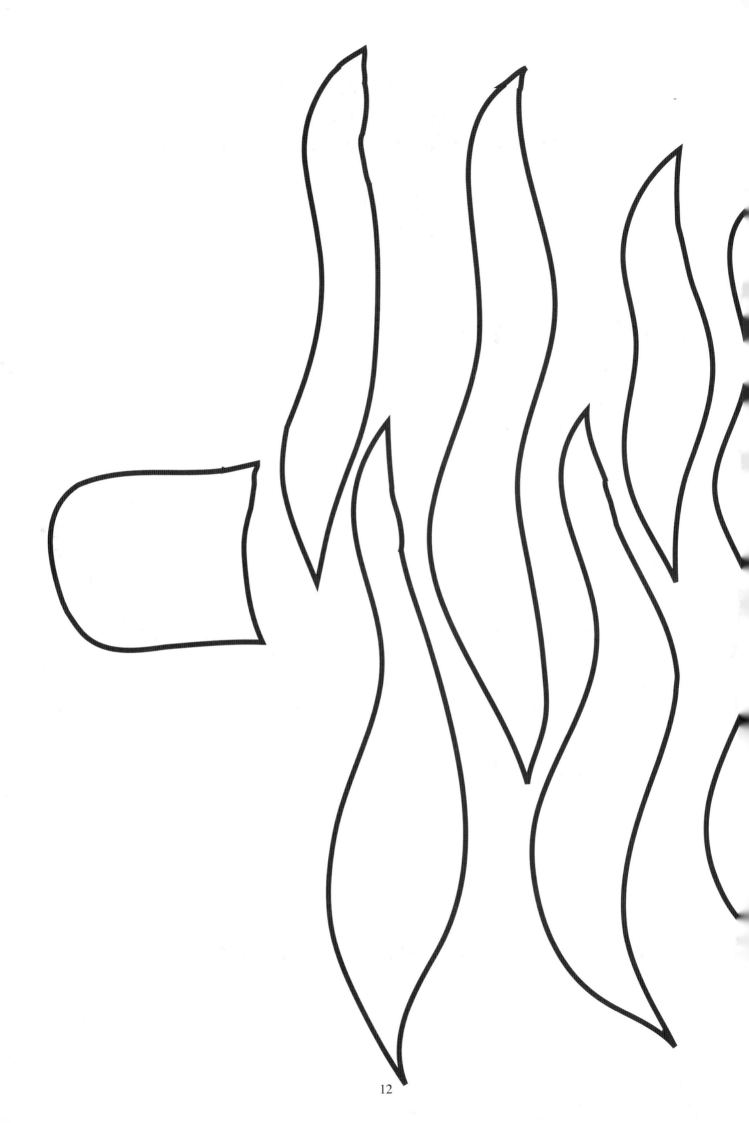

Christmas Tree wallhanging
Trace onto paper side of Bonda Web
Iron onto Wrong side of fabric paper side
up.
Tree is printed in reverse use photo on
front cover for fabric placement.

Take the 18 inch by 20 1/2 inch back panel and fold in 1/2 inch down one of the long sides and press fold, stitch with 1/4 inch seam.

On the same 2 edges fold over 1 inch and press again.

These are you zipper edges.

14. Take your zipper and the larger back panel and pin the folded edge right side up as close to the zipper teeth as you can get, starting 2 inches in from the zipper head. Leaving the zipper closed and using your zipper foot stitch as close to the folded edge as you can get.

Now take the other piece and place the folded edge over the zipper teeth covering the first row of stitching and pin in place. Using you zipper foot stitch down this side as close as you can get to the zipper.

Move the zipper head to the centre. Close the open end and stitch across to close.

15. Lay backing panel right side down and place the cushion panel on top right sides up.

Pin around the outer edge, cushion panel may be slightly smaller than the backing, centre it and pin and sew 1/8 th inch around the outer edge by machine and trim away any excess backing.

16. Take the 4 binding strips and join them together on the short ends to make one long strip. Fold in one end 1/2 inch and press. Fold the strip in half down the length and press the fold.

17. Starting with folded end of your binding in the middle of one side of your cushion front stitch the binding using 1/4 inch seam starting 1/2 inch from the end of your binding, with raw edges together.

Continue around your cushion, mitreing the corners, until you get back to where you started and stop 2 inches away from the start cut the excess binding leaving 1/2 inch overlap where they join. Slot the raw end inside the folded end and stitch over it to finish.

18. Fold binding over to back of cushion and hand stitch in place.

Heart and Star shapes for decorating gift bags

Window Shopping

**Made by
Sarah Wellfair
and
Helen Rymer**

**Finished size approx
17 inches wide
by 13 inches high by
4 inches deep**

Covered Notebooks

Requirements

Backing   **1 fat quarter**

Front   **3 fat quarters**

Binding   **1 fat quarter**

Wadding   **1/2 metre**
I use Warm and Natural

Thread for sewing and quilting

Spray glue (505 spray basting)

A6 Hard back note book

1. Cut one piece of backing fabric and wadding to 16 inches by 7 inches, spray glue the fabric to the wadding right side out.

2. Using a pen or pencil draw a line on the diagonal on the long sides somewhere in the centre of the wadding.

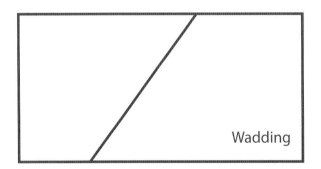

3. From the 3 Fat quarters cut strips in different sizes smallest 3/4 inch largest 1 1/2 inch, from each fabric.

4. Place one of the larger strips right side up along side the drawn line and pin in place.

5. Take one of the smaller strips and place right side together with the large strip lining up the edge with the drawn line.

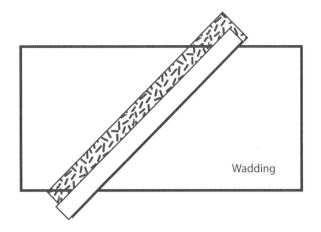

6. Stitch 1/4 inch seam through all layers, press the smaller strip over to cover the wadding.

7. Take another strip and place it on the same as before and pin and stitch in place, continue to add strips , flipping them over and pressing until you have covered one side of the wadding. Alternate colour and size of strips as you go.

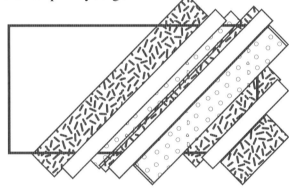

Turn it around and stitch and flip off the other side of the first strip to cover the remaining wadding.

8. It should now look like this.

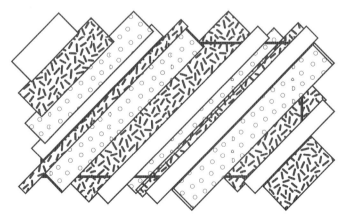

9. Using a rotary cutter and ruler cut to 15 inches by 7 inches.

It should now look like this.

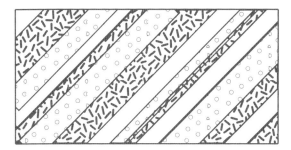

It should now look like this.

10. If you have decorative stitches on your machine you can stitch down the panels of fabric in a contrasting thread to decorate your book cover.

Stitching over ribbon is also very effective.
Pin the ribbon to the top edge of the book onto the strip of fabric you want to sew on and place it under the foot of the machine. Stitch decorative machine stitches over the ribbon to attach

11. From your binding fabric cut 2 pieces 2 1/4 inches by 7 inches, fold them in half down the length right sides out, press the fold and stitch to the short ends of your cover raw edge to raw edge on the short ends, using 1/4 inch seam allowance.

Fold them over to the back of your book cover and hand stitch to the backing.

12. Place the Book cover right sides down and measure 2 1/2 inches in from the short ends on both top and bottom long edges.

13 Fold the ends in on the 2 1/2 inch markers and pin in place.

It is a good idea to try the book in the cover to make sure it fits before you stitch it down.

Stitch across the top edges to hold them in place using 1/8th inch seam allowance.

I always reverse with the machine in the seam allowance where you go across the bound edges.

14. Cut two strips from your binding fabric 2 1/4 inches by 11 inches.

Fold binding in half right sides out and press fold.

15. Stitch binding onto the right side of the book cover with a 1/4 inch seam allowance, lining the raw edge of the binding with the top edge of the book cover, leaving 3/4 inch of binding hanging over each end.

Do the same to the bottom edge.

16. Flip the binding over to the back of the book cover and fold in the ends, hand stitch the binding over the stitch line to finish.

Place the book inside the cover you are now finished.

Any size book can be covered.

Measure the outer cover with the book closed. Add 1 1/2 inches to the width of the book and add enough to the length to fold to the inside cover so it covers half both sides of the book.

Cover can be trimmed to size after stitching.

Gift Bags

Finished size large bag 10 inches high by 10 1/2 inches wide by 5 inches deep approx.
Small bag 9 inches high by 10 inches wide by 4 1/2 inches deep approx.

Both bags are made up in the same way the sizes for the smaller bag are in brackets

Requirements

Main bag panel	**1 fat quarter**

Cut 2 pieces 11 inches wide by 8 1/2 inches
(10 inches wide by 7 1/2 inches)

Top contrast band and base	**1 fat quarter**

Top contrast

Cut 2 pieces 10 1/2 inches wide by 5 1/2 inches
(9 1/2 inches wide by 5 1/2 inches)

Base

Cut one piece 11 inches wide by 5 1/2 inches
(10 inches by 5 inches)

Bottom contrast and handles	**1 fat quarter**

Contrast

Cut 2 pieces 2 1/2 inches by 11 inches
(2 1/2 inches by 10 inches)

Handles the same for both bags

Cut 2 pieces 3 inches wide by required length
I have used approx 10 - 14 inches long.

Bag lining	**1 fat quarter**

Cut 2 pieces 10 1/2 inches wide by 10 inches
(9 1/2 inches wide by 9 inches)

From the remaining fabric cut one piece for the lining base.
5 inches by 10 1/2 inches
(9 1/2 inches by 4 1/2 inches)

1. Take the main bag panels and add the 2 1/2 inch base contrast to the bottom edge of both panels with 1/4 inch seam. If your main fabric is directional make sure they are the right way up.

2. Add the base panel to the base contrast panels.

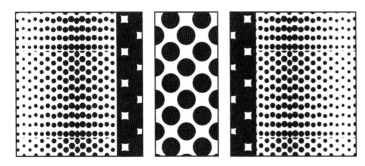

3. Lay bag panel onto cotton wadding and spray glue in place. If you want to appliqué hearts or stars on your bag now is the time to do them following the instructions for machine applique.

4. Quilt bag panel as required starting with stitching in the ditch along base seam, this line of stitching will give you a line to stitch on to form the base later.

I have quilted in random wavey lines across my main panel and straight lines on the base contrast and base panel.

5. Trim back wadding to edges of bag panel, I use my rotary cutter and ruler for this.

6. Fold bag in half right sides together and pin down the sides making sure you match the seams of the base contrast panels. Stitch down both sides with 1/4 inch seam.

7. Make base up the same as the Zen bag. Trim off corners. Turn bag right sides out.

8. Take the 2 lining panels and stitch to the base panel, using 1/4 inch seam allowance.

10. Place panel onto wadding and quilt as before starting with the base seams.

Trim away excess wadding and make bag lining up the same as the bag. Trim off the corners.

11.Place lining bag inside outer bag and pin around the top, starting at the side seams. Machine around the top 1/4 inch down with large machine stitch to hold in place.

12. Take the top contrast panels and fold in half down the length right sides out and press the fold.

13. Open them and place them right sides together and stitch down the short ends 1/4 inch seam. Fold in half on original fold right side out.

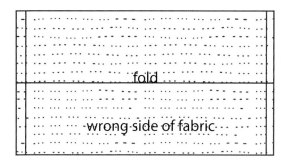

13. You should now have a hoop of fabric with a fold on one side and the two raw edges on the other side, it should be right sides out.

14. Place the hoop inside the bag with both raw edges in line with the top of the bag. Pin around the top starting at the side seams, use lots of pins for this as it will make it easier to handle when sewing in place.

15. Sew around the top of the bag with a generous 1/4 inch seam allowance, I always use the free arm on my machine to do this.

16. Pull the contrast hoop up over the top of the bag and stitch down along the bottom folded edge. You should now have a contrast top of approximately 2 inches outside and 1/4 inch inside. I always hand stitch the fold.

17. Take your handle strips and fold in half down the length right side out. Press fold.
Open out and fold raw edges into the centre fold you have just made. Press new folded edges.
Fold in half on original fold.
You should now have a strip a quarter the width of your original strip and with all raw edges hidden.
Stitch down the handle on the open edge first, then the folded edge. Add a few more lines down the centre or use a decorative embroidery stitch. The more stitching you do the stronger the handle will be.

18. Pin handles to the inside of the bag top 2 1/2 inches from the side seams and hand stitch in place. Sew buttons to outside of bag through the handles to add strength.

Your gift bag is now finished.

Christmas Tree
Finished size 20 1/2 inches by 25 1/2 inches

Requirements
Tree background   1 fat quarter of cream and gold fabric.
Cut one piece 14 1/2 inches by 18 1/2 inches.

Tree   1 fat quarter green and gold holly fabric

Inner border and binding   1 fat quarter of red spot fabric
Cut 2 pieces 1 1/2 inches 16 1/2 inches.
Cut 2 pieces 1 1/2 inches by 18 1/2 inches.

Cut 5 pieces 2 1/4 inches by 20 inches for binding.

Outer border   1 fat quarter of green patterned fabric.
Cut 4 pieces 20 1/2 inches by 2 1/2 inches.

Backing   60cm of cream fabric

Scrap of Brown Fabric for the tree trunk

Wadding   60 cm cotton wadding

1/2 metre of Bonda Web

Gold thread for applique

Red, cream and green thread for sewing and quilting.

Gold beads or small gold bells, and gold star button to decorate.

1. Trace the tree pattern onto the paper side of the Bonda Web. Place the Bonda Web, paper side up on the wrong side of your green tree fabric.
Iron in place, I always cover my pieces with parchment paper, if I make a mistake it will stick to my paper not my iron.

2. Trace the tree trunk onto Bonda Web and place on to a scrap of brown fabric, iron in place the same way you did the tree.

3. Layout your cream and gold background fabric, fold it in half down the length and gently press the fold, this will give you a centre line to line up your tree.

4. Carefully cut out the tree shapes and remove the paper backing. Starting at the top, place them right sides up, on the right side of the background.

The tree pattern is printed in reverse, you might find it easier to place the pieces if you use the finished tree picture.

5. Take time to position the pieces, using the centre fold as the centre of your tree. When you are happy with your placement cover with parchment paper and iron in place.

6. Take the 1 1/2 inch by 18 1/2 inch inner border pieces and add one to each side of the tree panel, using a 1/4 inch seam.

Press the seam allowance towards the border
Add the top and bottom inner border strips in the same way.

7. Take the outer border strips and sew them on in the same way.

Press the seam allowance towards the outer border.

8. Give the panel a final press.

9. Cut a piece of wadding and backing slightly larger than the panel.
Lay panel onto wadding and backing and spray glue or tack the three layers together.

10. Using gold thread on your machine stitch around the tree shape with a small zig-zag or button hole stitch. This will applique the shapes down and quilt through the 3 layers at the same time.

Stitch in the ditch around the centre panel and in the borders. I have stitched the background of the panel with random free motion quilting, the outer border has been quilted in lines 1/4 inch apart going round the centre panel.

Stitch star button to top of tree and beads to the ends of each tree section.

11. Trim back any excess wadding and backing ready to bind the edges.

12. Take the binding strips and join into one long strip. Fold the strip in half down the length and press the fold.

13. Measure across the centre of the piece and cut 2 pieces this length, stitch with 1/4 inch seam to the top and bottom edges of your wall hanging raw edges together on the front, fold binding over to the back and slip stitch in place on the back.

14. Measure top to bottom in the centre again and add 1 1/2 inches to this measurement, Stitch on as before leaving 3/4 inch over hang at both ends.

15. Fold binding over to the back as before, fold in the ends and slip stitch down to back .

16. Make a hanging sleeve and hand stitch on to the back at the top.

Your Christmas tree wall hanging is finished.

Drawstring bag

Finished size 8 x 8 x 15 inches

Requirements

Centre square on pockets   4 x 3 1/2 inch square
I have used Makower labels

Pockets inner border   1 fat quarter
Cut 8 pieces 3 1/2 inches by 1 1/2 inches
Cut 8 pieces 5 1/2 inches by 1 1/2 inches

Pockets Outer border   1 fat quarter
Cut 8 pieces 5 1/2 inches by 2 inches
Cut 8 pieces 8 1/2 inches by 2 inches

Pocket lining   1 fat quarter
Cut 4 pieces 8 1/2 inches by 9 inches

Outer bag   2 fat quarters
Cut 2 pieces from each fat quarter 16 inches by 8 1/2 inches.

Inner bag   1/2 metre or
**   2 fat quarters**
Cut 4 pieces 16 inches by 8 1/2 inches

1/2 metre of wadding
Cut 6 pieces 8 1/2 inches square, 4 for the pockets and 2 for the base

1/2 metre of quilters flannel
Cut 4 pieces 16 inches by 8 1/2 inches

Thread for sewing and quilting

From the remaining fabric cut 2 pieces 8 1/2 inches square for the inner and outer base.

Cut 2 pieces 2 inches wide by 36 inches long, you may need to join fabric to get the length. These are your drawstrings.

1. Take the centre squares and add one 3 1/2 inch strip to the top and bottom of each square with 1/4 inch seam. Press seam towards the border.

Add 2 of the 5 1/2 inch strips to either side with 1/4 inch seam, press as before.

2. Add the next border strips in the same way. Press seams towards the outer edges.

Pocket panels should now look like this.

Lay each pocket panel onto a square of wadding. Place the pocket linings right side together with the pocket front, lining up the top edge. Stitch across the top edge with a 1/4 inch seam.

Take the lining up over the top to the back of the pocket leaving 1/4 inch showing on the front of the pocket, giving it a contrast edge, press in place. Stitch in the ditch along the top contrast. Quilt pocket panels.

3. Take the outer bag panels and mark the centre of the top short edge, if you are using a directional fabric make sure it is the right way up. Measure down the sides 4 inches and mark. Using a ruler and cutter, line up the marks and cut off the corners.

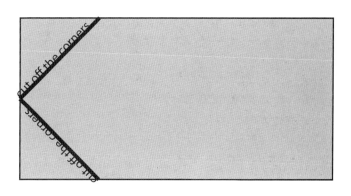

4. These points are at the top of your pocket.

Measure down from the marks on the side 1 inch and draw a line across, draw a second line 1 inch below on all four panels. this will make the casing for your drawstrings later.

Place a pocket on each panel right side out. Pin in place.

5. Stitch down the sides and along the bottom edge of the pockets with 1/8 th inch seam.

Do all the panels the same.

5. Take the 8 1/2 inch base panels and place them right side up onto the remaining 8 1/2 inch squares of wadding. Quilt the 2 base panels.

5. Take one side panel at a time and line up the bottom edge with one side of the base panel right sides together. Pin in place, start stitch 1/4 inch in from the end with 1/4 inch seam allowance, finishing 1/4 inch form the other end.

6. Add the other 3 sides in the same way, alternating the 2 different fabrics.

It should now look like this.

7. Taking one side at a time pin the two pieces right sides together, I always pin the top of the pocket first to line them up. Stitch down the side with 1/4 inch seam reverse over the top of the pocket to add strength.

8. Do the remaining sides the same. Turn the bag right side out.

9. Take the lining pieces and the 4 pieces of quilters flannel the same size. Place the fabric panels onto the flannel pieces, measure and cut the tops the same as for the outer bag. I usually spray glue these together with 505.

10. Make up the inner bag the same as the outer bag, leaving a 4 inch gap in the stitching on one side seam. This is to turn the bag through later.

11. Place the outer bag into the inner bag right sides together. Pin the two together, side seams first, then the points and finally the sides of the pointed top.

12. Carefully stitch around the top with a 1/4 inch seam.

13. Trim off the points being careful not to cut the stitching and snip in the dips where the side seams meet.

14. Turn the bag carefully through the gap in the side

seam, use the end of a pencil and gently push the points out. Push the lining inside the bag and make it fit. Roll the top seam of the bag between your fingers until it is on the edge, Press the top edge and pin.

15. Top stitch around the top 1/4 inch in. Hand stitch the gap in the side seam closed.

16. Carefully pin around the drawn lines, pining the 3 layers together.

17. Stitch around the bag on both the drawn lines, if you reverse over the side seams it will add strength. These are the casings for your drawstrings, carefully on two opposite sides snip the stitches in the side seam on the outside of the bag between the casings, this is to feed the drawstrings through.

18. Take your drawstring strips and fold in half down the length right side out. Press fold.
Open out and fold raw edges into the centre fold you have just made. Press new folded edges.
Fold in half on original fold.
You should now have a strip a quarter the width of your original strip and with all raw edges hidden.
Stitch down the drawstring on the open edge first, then the folded edge.

19. Take one drawstring and thread through one of the side seams into the casing, thread it all the way round and back out the same hole, tie the two ends together in a knot. Take the remaining drawstring and thread it through the hole in the opposite seam and take it all the way round and back out the same hole, tie as before.

20. The bag should now close when both strings are pulled at the same time.

Dazzle Quilt
Finished size approx 58 inches by 40 inches
Requirements
6 fat quarters of contrasting fabric
From each fat quarter cut 3 pieces 5 1/2 inches by 21 inches.
Long quarter for inner border
From this cut 5 pieces 1 1/2 inches by the length.
3/4 metre for outer border
From this cut 5 pieces 5 inches by the length.
Long quarter for binding
From this cut 5 pieces 2 inches by the length
45 inches by 60 inches cotton wadding
1 1/2 metres of fabric for backing.

1. Take one of each colour from the fat quarter strips and sew into row of six strips down the length.

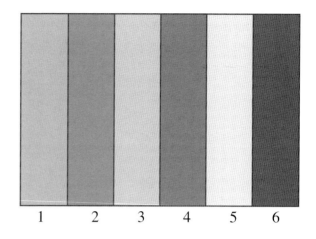

2. Press all the seam allowances in one direction.

Fold in half right sides together and lay it flat, sew strip one to strip 6 . You should now have a hoop of fabric strips.

3. Flatten the hoop with a seam top and bottom.

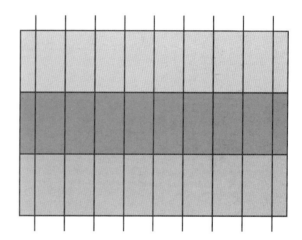

4. Straighten the left edge of your hoop. Cut 8 tubes 2 1/2 inches wide from your piece.

5. Do the same with the other fat quarter strips.

6. You should now have 24 fabric tubes.

7. The pattern is made up of alternating rows.

8. Take hoop 1 and cut off the seam allowance between fabric 1 and fabric 6 on the stitch line and lay out the strip.

9. Take hoop 2 and fold fabric 1 in half and match the seams, cut on the fold. Lay strip 2 down under strip 1, these two strips make up the pattern.

10. Repeat with the rest of the strips, sew together in pairs and then sew the pairs together to make the centre panel of the quilt

Your panel should now look like this. Press all seams in one direction

11. Take the inner border strips and join then into one long piece.

12. Measure down the centre of your quilt and cut 2 pieces to this length and sew then to the side of your quilt panel with 1/4 inch seam allowance. Press seam allowance towards the border.

13. Now measure your quilt across the middle and cut 2 pieces to this length and sew to the top and the bottom with same 1/4 inch seam allowance, press seam allowance towards the border.

14. Now do the same with the outer border strips.

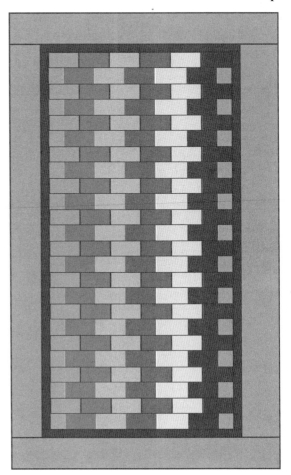

15. Press the quilt well and lay onto wadding and backing. Spray glue or pin layers together, quilt panel.

16. Trim wadding and backing back to edges of quilt.

17. Sew the binding strips into one long piece, fold it in half right side out down the length and press the fold.

18. Measure down the centre of your quilt and cut 2 binding strips to this size, stitch them to the side edges of your quilt on the front raw edge to raw edge with 1/4 inch seam. Flip these over to the back and slip stitch down on the backing.

19. Measure across the middle of your quilt and add on 1 1/2 inches to this measurement, Stitch to the top and bottom of your quilt leaving 3/4 inch over each end.

20. Flip the binding over to the back and fold in the ends and slip stitch down to the backing as before.

Your quilt is now finished.